IMAGES
of England

THE
LEEDS & LIVERPOOL
CANAL IN YORKSHIRE

Springs Canal at Skipton, 1928.

British Waterways – 2,000 miles of history

British Waterways runs the country's two-centuries-old working heritage of canals and river navigations. It conserves the historic buildings, structures and landscapes which blend to create the unique environment of the inland waterways, and protects their valuable and varied habitats.

As part of its commitment to the heritage of the waterways, British Waterways was instrumental in setting up The Waterways Trust, which aims to educate the public about the inland waterways and to promote the restoration and preservation of their rich architectural, historical and environmental heritage.

The Waterways Trust is a partnership between British Waterways, The National Waterways Museum at Gloucester, the Boat Museum at Ellesmere Port and the Canal Museum, Stoke Bruerne. The Trust cares for the National Waterways Collection, the country's pre-eminent collection of canal artefacts, documents and boats which are on view to the public at all the museums.

The Waterways Trust also manages the British Waterways Archive, a unique collection of inland waterway records dating back to the late seventeenth century and containing the largest documentary and photographic resource of its kind in Britain. Supported by the Heritage Lottery Fund, the archive is the subject of an ambitious project to make the collection available to all via the Internet. The new Cyber Archive will, for the first time, create a single catalogue of Britain's canal archives, revolutionizing research into the history of the inland waterways.

For more information about British Waterways call 01923 20 11 20 or visit the website at www.britishwaterways.co.uk.

For access to the archive, or to get up-to-date information about the Cyber Archive project, call 01452 318041.

IMAGES
of England

THE
LEEDS & LIVERPOOL
CANAL IN YORKSHIRE

Dr Gary Firth

To Fatman and Dibby,
two intrepid towpath walkers

TEMPUS

Five Rise Locks, Bingley.

First published 1999
Reprinted 2003

Tempus Publishing Limited
The Mill, Brimscombe Port,
Stroud, Gloucestershire, GL5 2QG
www.tempus-publishing.com

British Library Cataloguing in Publication Data.
A catalogue record for this book is available from the British Library.

ISBN 0 7524 1631 6

Typesetting and origination by Tempus Publishing Limited
Printed in Great Britain by Midway Colour Print, Wiltshire

Contents

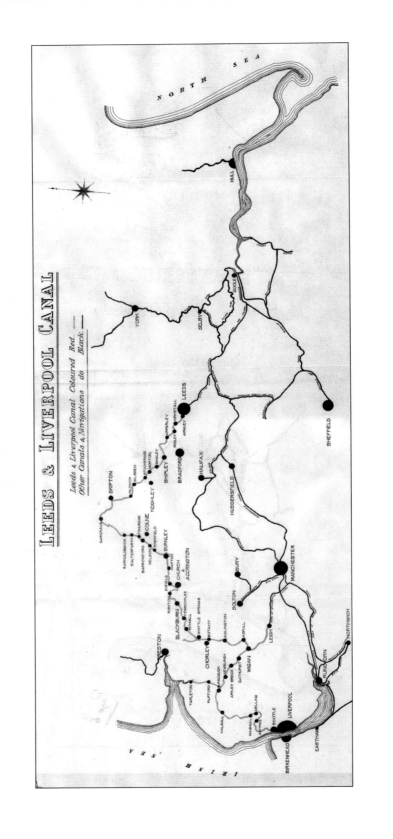

Introduction
The Origins of the Leeds & Liverpool

By 1720 the capacity of Britain's natural system of inland waterways had been almost fully realized. Pioneering schemes, like the Aire & Calder Navigation in Yorkshire (1699) and the Douglas Navigation (1742) in Lancashire, had served crucial areas of developing industry by moving bulky goods and materials more quickly and cheaply than ever before. Waterways were the answer to Britain's logistics problem but they were often too shallow, too narrow and too difficult to access. By 1750 it was logical to move towards the idea of artificial and man-made waterways in response to the rising populations of provincial towns and their needs of food and fuel.

On the Yorkshire side of the Pennines the expanding West Riding textile towns of Leeds, Wakefield and Bradford were trading heavily in wool, imported corn and minerals, like coal and limestone. The problems of moving large amounts of heavy materials, like coal, from the mines into growing ports and towns like Hull and Manchester, had been engaging the minds of Northern merchants and landowners throughout the first half of the eighteenth century.

Mike Clarke, the official historian of the Leeds & Liverpool Canal, has written:

> The Merchants in the west-coast ports of Glasgow, Liverpool and Bristol, who traded with the American colonies, wanted to sell their colonial produce in the rich markets in the east of the country and in Europe. At the same time the manufacturers from the east wanted to enter the expanding Liverpool market. To allow this trade to develop, good cross country links were needed. Eventually the provision of these routes went some considerable way towards integrating the economies of east and west.'

The idea of building a cross-country waterway has its origins in the decades of the mid-eighteenth century, following the exploitation of the Wigan coalfield by the Duke of Bridgewater and his canal in 1759-1760. This man-made waterway, crossing the River Irwell by means of the Barton aqueduct, dramatically reduced the cost of coal in Manchester, prompting the Duke to comment 'that a good canal should have coals at the heels of it.' This truism was equally appropriate to the eastern side of the Pennines where John Stanhope was one of a dozen colliery owners mining coal around Bradford.

Stanhope was a leading lawyer on the Northern Circuit. His reputation had spread beyond the York and Lancaster Assizes as far as London with his handling of the case of the Leeds cloth merchants against the stamping and measurement of woollen cloth. More importantly he was Lord of the manors of Horsforth and Thornton where he worked several collieries from his headquarters at Horsforth Low Hall.

It was there, on a summer morning in June 1765, that he received a letter from his twenty-one year-old nephew Walter who was about to undertake the Grand Tour. With an eye to early tourism, the Duke of Bridgewater had encouraged important travellers to visit his coal mines at Worsley and the famous aqueduct at Barton. Young Walter, whose inheritance included several furnaces, forges and slitting mills on his grandfather's estate at Cannon Hall in South Yorkshire, was inevitably drawn to Bridgewater's successful commercial scheme and immediately informed his uncle of his favourable impressions of the visit.

An extract from the letter sent to John Stanhope by his nephew Walter, in which he expressed his admiration for the Bridgewater Canal.

John Stanhope, no doubt influenced by his nephew's letter, was already contemplating the proposal of a linkage of the river Aire with the river Ribble at Preston (1764) and, within weeks of receiving the letter, he had hired John Longbotham to survey a route 'to link the East and West Seas'. It was Stanhope who convened the first public meeting in Bradford on 2 July 1766 to promote a trans-Pennine waterway. Three years later he topped the list of over a hundred subscribers to a fund for making a complete plan and costing of the canal scheme from Preston (not Liverpool!) to join with the Aire & Calder Navigation at Leeds. A Yorkshire Canal Committee, led by Stanhope, requested the canal engineer James Brindley to confirm Longbotham's route of the waterway and to accept the need of 'a large canal', broad enough to receive vessels already using the Douglas and Aire & Calder Navigations (i.e. boats 60ft long by 14ft beam, which were already working the tidal Humber River as far as Hull).

In December 1768 the Lancashire and Yorkshire committees met in Burnley where Brindley estimated the cost of the proposed canal at £259,777 and recommended £100 shares with interest at 5%. There was already disquiet at this meeting from the Lancashire committee who were not happy with the line of the canal bypassing the coalfields of South Lancashire, particularly Wigan. The Lancastrians renewed their complaint that the line went too far north and contracted John Eyres and Richard Melling to plan a separate line to satisfy their needs.

By the autumn of 1769 John Stanhope was terminally ill and slowly handed over the initiative of the scheme to John Hustler, also of Bradford. In October of that year Hustler asked Brindley to decide upon the final route, flatly refusing to finance any other surveys out of the subscription fund which had reached over £150,000. The Longbotham line was preferred by Brindley and, as a result, many Lancashire subscribers immediately withdrew. Fearing further defections, Hustler chose to promote the Bill in London and the Bill became law in May 1770. At the first general meeting, (held when Stanhope had already died) a committee of twenty-three was elected, including several Bradford mine owners and Hustler was elected treasurer. Brindley was appointed chief engineer and Longbotham clerk of works, although Longbotham fulfilled both roles on Brindley's death in 1772.

Building began at both ends of the line and, by March 1774, the line from Skipton to Thackley, near Shipley, was finished, together with the difficult stretch from Bingley to Shipley. This included the famous staircase locks of Bingley Five Rise which required a plentiful supply of water. These, and the nearby Three Rise Locks, were engineered by Longbotham and built by local masons. They were officially opened on 21 March 1774 when a boat carrying coal passed through in twenty-eight minutes. The event was given full coverage in the regional press, *Leeds Intelligencer*:

From Bingley to about three miles downwards the noblest works of the kind...are exhibited viz.: A fivefold, a threefold, a twofold and a single lock, making together a fall of 120ft; a large aqueduct bridge of seven arches over the River Aire and an aqueduct and banking over the Shipley Valley... This joyful and much wished for event was welcomed with the ringing of Bingley bells, a band of music, the firing of guns by the neighbouring Militia, the shouts of the spectators, and all the marks of satisfaction that so important an acquisition merits.

At the western end of the canal a link with the Douglas Navigation was completed when the Leeds & Liverpool Canal Company bought out that line, giving access to the Wigan Coalfield. Coal from the Douglas Valley 'became the lifeblood of this important and profitable waterway.' The building of a short branch canal from Shipley to Bradford (1774) was equally important for Bradford's economic development. Bradford colliery owners had subscribed an inordinately large amount of capital to the Leeds & Liverpool Canal scheme and, by building the branch canal to Bradford they were able to utilize a national subscription fund to promote and finance beneficial trading connections within their own regional economy. In particular, John Hustler had been able to maximize his religious connections with the wealthy Quaker communities in London and Norwich. In the early years of the company its affairs were run very much in the interests of Bradford where the company's head office was located until 1850. John Eagles, a Bradford solicitor, became the company law clerk and Bradford's John Hustler became sole treasurer until his death in 1790.

By October 1775 the Yorkshire side of the canal had been extended from Skipton to Gargrave and the link with the Aire & Calder Navigation at Leeds was completed in June 1777. The importance of coal and lime traffic on the eastern side of the Leeds & Liverpool Canal was confirmed by an expanding and profitable trade in those materials from an early date, particularly

John Hustler, who succeeded his father, John, as a director of the canal and was later treasurer of the Leeds & Liverpool Canal Company.

The Leeds & Liverpool Canal Company's Head Office.

with the construction of the Bradford Canal and the Spring's Canal (1773) at Skipton. The latter was built and financed by Lord Thanet, proprietor of Skipton Castle and limestone quarries close by. This short canal was leased by the Leeds & Liverpool Company from 1785. By that time, seventy-five miles of canal had been built at a cost of £232,016 and henceforth the company was forced to borrow to complete the scheme. At the time of the War of American Independence government stock was a much more attractive investment than canals and, as a result, all building work on the canal ceased. This period of inactivity allowed the Lancashire merchants to reconsider the route through south Lancashire. Consequently an Act was passed in 1790 authorising extra capital to implement an alternative route, taking in the growing south Lancashire cotton towns of Blackburn and Burnley.

Traffic quickly increased on both sides of the Pennines, particularly in coal, and by 1774 Yorkshire had twenty-six of the seventy-five boats in operation along the canal. The income from each side of the Pennines was relative to the number of boats. The main carrier on the Yorkshire side in the early years was Messrs Preston, Hird and Co., who became lessors of the Bradford Canal Company and proprietors of the Bradford Limekiln Company as well as major shareholders in the large Low Moor Ironworks at Bradford.

As the British financial climate improved after 1786, Hustler and his fellow directors made a determined effort to complete the canal by raising loans and authorising some major engineering projects on the newly agreed line. These included the Foulridge Tunnel (1796) of 1,640 yards and the mile-long Burnley embankment. These late developments were mainly on the Lancashire side whereas the Yorkshire route was very much completed by 1777.

In October 1816 the Leeds & Liverpool Canal was finally completed at a cost of £877,616, considerably more than Brindley's original estimate. It had taken forty-six years to build and was 127 miles long. There were forty-four locks on the Yorkshire side and forty-seven in Lancashire and more than 300 bridges along its route. The first company barge to travel the entire route left Leeds on Saturday 19 October 1816 and arrived in Liverpool the following Wednesday, receiving a tumultuous reception all the way.

One
The Route (i)

The one hundred and twenty-seven and a quarter miles of the Leeds & Liverpool Canal make it the longest single canal in Great Britain. Its eastern terminus is at Leeds where the canal locks into the Aire & Calder Navigation, thus completing a trans-Pennine waterway between the River Mersey in the west and the ports of the Humber estuary in the east.

The canal leaves the centre of Leeds passing under the Leeds and Thirsk Railway Bridge and the Wellington Road bridge. At Spring Garden Lock the canal rises 9ft and runs along a sandstone scarp above the River Aire towards Armley and Kirkstall. Leaving the riverside fields of Kirkstall Abbey and passing through Kirkstall Lock, the canal is now approximately 120ft above mean sea level. Three-rise locks at Kirkstall Forge and Newlay lift the canal almost 50ft above sea level and take it past Bramley Fall Woods.

Passing under Newlay Bridge, the line of the canal curves sharply southwards parallel to the course of the River Aire. The towpath continues towards Rodley, a true canal community where there are moorings, boatyards and a swing bridge. From Rodley the canal, river and railway follow a pleasantly wooded route through central Airedale towards Apperley Bridge, with its British Waterways offices and the attractive twin locks of Dobson Locks. At Apperley Bridge the canal curves northwards to follow the line of the River Aire towards Esholt and Thackley, where it passes under the railway which enters Thackley Tunnel. In order to avoid the steep wooded hill, the canal and the river are forced north-westwards, through Buck Woods towards Idle and Shipley where the redundant junction with the Bradford Canal (1774) can be seen at Windhill.

Once past the Shipley Wharf, with its pleasure cruiser centre and restaurants, the canal follows the main river valley westwards to the model village of Saltaire. Beyond Titus Salt's Utopia the line of the canal passes through Hirst Woods, an ancient birch and oak wood on a glacial moraine above the river, which runs beneath the canal at this point via the Seven Arches aqueduct at Dowley Gap where twin locks raise the canal 18ft 4in. The canal rises even more sharply on the stretch at Bingley where the famous Five Rise Locks were considered a wonder of the eighteenth-century world. These and the nearby Three Rise Locks raise the canal 89ft 11in. Leaving the town of Bingley where canal, river, road and railway converge in a narrow gorge, the canal moves out into open countryside where it skirts high along the valley side with panoramic views up and down this beautiful part of Airedale.

For cyclists and boat owners, etc., there now commences a long, relatively level, stretch of the water westwards to Skipton passing Micklethwaite and Riddlesden where there is a small warehousing area at Stockbridge and wharfage at Granby Lane. The canal next bypasses the town of Keighley, although a branch canal was considered in 1821. The canal follows its north-westerly course in the winding valley between moorland, woodland and valley bottom farmland; passing the links of Keighley Golf Club (scene of a huge breach in 1952) towards the commuter belt of Silsden where there is a marina and wharf in the heart of the old industrial village.

The eastern terminus of the Leeds & Liverpool Canal is in the heart of the city of Leeds where the canal connects with the Aire & Calder Navigation leading to Hull and other ports of the Humber estuary. Here is a view of the docks on the River Aire below Leeds Bridge, c.1900. A female bargee guides her empty vessel to the head of the Aire & Calder Navigation.

A similar view, with the *Mary* of Bingley being shafted downriver towards the Navigation Company docks. This barge was owned by John Barron & Sons, coal merchants of Bingley, and was likely to load up with coal from the South Yorkshire coalfield for distribution to the industrial towns of the Aire Valley. The large warehouse in the centre has recently been converted into pleasant waterside accommodation. Adjoining it to the left is the cement and plaster works of H.D. Atkinson and to the right in the distance is the imposing tower of St Peter's Leeds parish church.

A view of Leeds Bridge itself, *c*.1914 with a steam tug heading upstream towards the canal junction with a coal boat in tow. Steam towage on this stretch of the river, between the two waterways, was introduced in 1866 by the Airedale Tug Company.

The River Aire at Leeds shortly before its junction with the canal. The Aire & Calder Navigation had received parliamentary approval in 1699 and was completed in 1704. Its boats imported corn into West Yorkshire from East Anglia and coal from South Yorkshire. Other major commodities were wool and limestone. Here, a boat loaded with merchandise is prepared for its journey westwards.

The terminus of the Leeds & Liverpool Canal at Leeds where the River Aire locks into the canal (left of picture). On the right, a Leeds Co-op boat, the *Alice M. Thompson*, is tied up at the Co-op's wharf on the Aire where a steam crane is loading coal. In the background the railway viaduct (originally Leeds & Bradford 1846) crosses canal company property. *c.*1955.

A later picture (*c.*1960) of the same scene showing the first (or last) lock on the canal at its junction with the River Aire. In the right foreground, another Co-op boat loaded with coal. Beyond it, a new boat under construction in Rider's boatyard. To the left of the picture is the original warehouse (1770) of the Leeds & Liverpool Canal Company.

The terminus office of the Leeds & Liverpool Canal on the eastern side of the Pennines at the Canal Basin, Leeds. Erected in a classical style, this office was built as a meeting room for John Hustler and his fellow directors of the company in 1770, but later became a toll office when the Company headquarters moved to Bradford.

A touch of Tuscany. Close to the canal company's offices are these two fine Italianate factory towers. They were originally part of the premises of T.W. Harding, c.1863. The tower on the right, with the octagonal top, is a copy of the campanile of the Palazzo della Signoria in Verona and was built as a chimney in 1864. The other tower is modelled on Giotto's campanile of 1334 at the Duomo in Florence and was erected in 1899 in order to extract iron dust from the works' grinding wheels.

The old Half-Moon Bridge above Office Lock. The bridge was demolished in 1961.

Unloading sand at Leeds in 1955.

Monk Bridge. Another crossing of the canal and river close to the centre of Leeds. This one carries the old Leeds-Halifax turnpike road. The original bow-spring tied bridge, made at Bowling Ironworks, Bradford, was replaced by this bridge in 1886. The Leeds coat of arms can just be seen within the decorated spandrel of the arch.

Giant's Hill. Here the canal runs along a sandstone scarp well above the River Aire. On this lofty site stood the remains of a Norman motte and bailey Castle, substantially intact until the canal was cut through here in 1792.

The Leeds-Thirsk railway viaduct carries the railway across the Aire Valley and the canal by means of a succession of arches. This arch spanning the canal is particularly well proportioned with niches in the flanking piers – on the left – and perfectly balanced wedges of stone making up the arch over the canal. A beautiful piece of railway architecture over an inland waterway.

Armley Mills. Here the segmented stone bridge over the canal dates from the 1770s and gives access from the south to the Armley Mills (now Leeds Industrial Museum). Most of the present mill was built between 1804 and 1805 by Benjamin Gott, the great Leeds merchant and industrialist.

Redcote Branch. This short water 'lay-by' alongside the canal makes an island of the canal towpath (right). It was constructed in 1927 to receive coal barges serving the now defunct Kirkstall Power Station. Here, barges and pleasure craft are moored as weekend retreats.

Redcote Bridge. A pleasure craft heading towards the centre of Leeds passes under the canal bridge which carried the former drive to Benjamin Gott's country mansion, Armley House. Between 1810 and 1822 he changed the appearance of the whole area, redesigning both the house and its parkland to the highest standards. The famous landscape designer Humphrey Repton was contracted to re-fashion the estate with some magnificent views towards Kirkstall and Leeds.

Kirkstall Lock, 121ft above mean sea level. This single lock is located alongside the ancient river meadows of Kirkstall Abbey (visible in the distance), a daughter house of Fountains Abbey and built by the Cistercians in 1152. This romantic and picturesque stretch of the canal was favoured by eighteenth-century water colourists like Turner and Thomas Girtin.

Forge Locks, Kirkstall. This set of three riser locks raises the canal $23\frac{1}{2}$ft. To the north, in the distance, is Kirkstall Forge founded by the Spencer family in the seventeenth century. Its power came from the medieval goit which ran down to the monastic mill pond. This watercourse powered tilt hammers and a slitting mill by means of two undershot cast-iron waterwheels.

Below: Newlay Locks, 1906. Another three-rise set of locks at Newlay raise the canal to 177ft above sea level. They were replaced at Easter time in 1906. The repair boat is the company's steamer *Ada*. In the centre is a young lady who should be elsewhere. Perhaps she is eager to display her Easter bonnet.

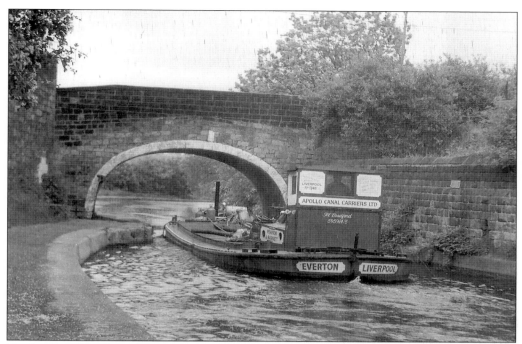

Newlay Canal Bridge is the backdrop to the *Everton*, a 'town' class craft built in 1953 by Harland & Woolf for British Transport Waterways. By 1979 the boat was on hire to Apollo Canal Carriers Ltd for the last regular intensive cargo carrying operation on the canal (to date).

Rodley Crane Works. An all too familiar sight along Britain's waterways in the 1960s and 1970s. Redundant industries left behind a trail of dereliction and neglect. However, with the amenity value of the canal being finally recognized, perhaps these old buildings of the Rodley Crane Works can be found a new lease of life for the future. The works were founded in 1820 to provide hand-operated cranes, stone-cutting equipment and winches for the local quarry industry. After 1860, the firm concentrated on the production of steam cranes and excavators for work on projects like the Manchester Ship Canal, the London Underground, the Zambesi Bridge and the Aswan Dam.

The port, Rodley, c.1900. A horse-drawn coal boat, having discharged its load, is now setting off to turn (wind) probably at the 'winding hole' just above Calverley Bridge, by the gasworks.

Rodley. A typical canalside community spawned by the coming of the canal in 1777. Its solid stone built houses run down to the south bank of the canal and originally included a canal pub, the Rodley Barge, a company warehouse and coal wharf and extensive stabling for the horses.

Apperley Bridge, 1954. Two empty coal barges return to Leeds on the Apperley Bridge stretch of the canal in 1954. There, the company located one of its major boatyards on the eastern side of the Pennines where company maintenance boats were built and repaired. Coffins were also made there for long-serving company employees who had died. Their movement along the canal had priority over all other traffic.

Apperley Locks, 1955. Locally known as Dobson Locks, these two riser locks lifted the canal over 20ft. The stretch of canal between Leeds and Skipton was completed by 1777 and in those early days engineers made extensive use of staircase locks like those at Apperley, Newlay and Kirkstall. The best examples are at Bingley (Five and Three Rise). Riser locks used more water than frequent single locks and for this reason were not used so often on later stretches of the canal where water was at a premium. Here a maintenance diver has just submerged as colleagues pump air to him.

A breach at Apperley Bridge, 1958. The canal has burst its banks and the water finds its way back into the River Aire.

Swing bridge, Bottom Farm. Here the canal passes beneath the former Midland Railway at Bottom Farm, Idle. The young man on the bridge points to the train about to enter Thackley Tunnel which took the railway line through the steeply wooded hillside on the right, known as the Nosegay.

The Nosegay, Idle. This hillside of mixed woodland is bypassed by the canal (and river) following the natural contours of the local terrain. This is a good example of the early (1776) canal engineers keeping to the contours rather than tunnelling through the hillside at great cost in time and money. Here the canal bends to the left in the direction of Buck Woods and Shipley.

Rockcliffe Farm, Idle, c.1935. A horse-drawn boat passes the ancient farmstead at Rockcliffe, or Rawcliffe, on its way to Leeds.

Buck Woods, Thackley, 1937. The horse-drawn boat *New Era* is towed through the swing bridge at Buck Woods. The boat was owned by Canal Carriers Ltd of Shipley.

Windhill Junction. At Dock Bridge, Windhill, the Leeds & Liverpool Canal is joined by the Bradford Canal (left). The white-washed building on the left is Junction House accommodating the toll office and boatmen's lodging house. This building was occupied for a number of years by T. & W.H. Clark, millwrights and engineers. Junction Mill in the background marks the importance of wool textiles to Shipley and this part of Airedale. The bridge was built to take the towpath from the south bank of the canal to the north.

Windhill, c.1955. Another view of the Windhill Junction again looking from the south side of the Leeds & Liverpool Canal towards Bradford. Junction House again to the right and, in the distance on the left, Dixon's Buildings.

Dixon's Buildings, c.1880. The warehouse premises of Shipley engineers W.P. Butterfield and the Great Northern Hardware Works alongside the Bradford Canal (left) shortly before it joins the Leeds & Liverpool Canal. The boat is loading goods directly from the warehouse beneath Windhill Bridge.

Glover's Wharf, Shipley c.1960. Another canalside community mushroomed here after Joseph Glover erected the premises on the left of this photograph, c.1815. Glover was a carpenter and early carrier on the canal. He provided stabling and warehousing at this point. To the right a maintenance boat is moored outside Harry Binn's cottage close to Gallows Bridge.

Unloading coal at Shipley, c.1900. It was much quicker and easier to fill a coal boat than it was to unload it. The ancient method of shovel and wheelbarrow continued well into the twentieth century along the whole line of the canal and applies here at Shipley Wharf in 1900.

Shipley Wharf, c.1975. Here the canal passes the premises of the engineering works of J. Parkinson & Son Ltd, who were making and exporting looms and spinning machines here as early as 1893. After 1918 they became famous for their precision tool-making, including milling machines, gear cutters and their world-famous industrial vices. Shipley's numerous engineering businesses expanded as the textile trade contracted.

Wharf Street, Shipley, c.1935. On the completion of the railway lease, a full survey of the Canal Company's warehouses was made in 1873. Those at Shipley were in sore need of improvement, along with Stockbridge, Kirkstall and Rodley. These, in Wharf Street, Shipley, were for wool storage but have recently been upgraded for leisure purposes, including a gym club, restaurant and bar. The house in the centre became the offices of Canal Carriers Ltd.

Victoria Bridge, Shipley, 1936. A view of the canal basin and warehouses at Shipley on a misty November morning in 1936. The barges are carrying coal. The photograph is taken from Victoria Bridge (Mason's Bridge).

The canal basin, Shipley, 1989. The same view as the previous illustration, now the headquarters of Apollo Canal Cruises, and several of their passenger boats: *Apollo*, *Hebble* and *Water Prince*. For several years they have operated the Metro-Waterbus on the canal between Shipley and Bingley, with a regular timetable in the summer months and special dinner cruises.

Jane Hills, c.1960. This cluster of buildings dating from 1796 to the mid-nineteenth century is immediately adjacent to the towpath on the north bank of the canal between Shipley Wharf and the model industrial village of Saltaire. The gable end of the original building (on the left of the picture) has a loom workshop with a blocked taking-in door. At one time it is thought a boatmen's lodging house occupied the site on the right of the photograph, although the 1881 census shows only one 'sailor' living here at that time. The path in the foreground is the canal towpath.

Salt's Mill, Saltaire, 1936. These are possibly company maintenance boats, Leeds-bound at Saltaire during the inter-war years.

Hirst Lock, *c.*1920. This single lock at Hirst Wood raises the canal 10ft 2in to a height of 216ft above sea level. In the background is the lock-keeper's cottage and Mr Whincup's Hirst Farm. To the right is the ancient Shipley settlement of the Hyrst.

Hirst Mill Bridge, *c.*1935. The swing bridge over the canal at Hirst Lock shows the lock-keeper's cottage in 1935 which was demolished shortly afterwards. In the far distance is Saltaire. From here the canal passes through a picturesque ancient woodland of oak and birch between a glacial moraine and the river.

Seven Arches Aqueduct. At the western end of Hirst Wood this long aqueduct of seven arches carries the canal 30ft above the River Aire as it winds around glacial boulder gravel. The aqueduct was built by local stonemasons James Rhodes of Shipley, Jonathon Sykes of Oulton and Joseph Smith of Woodlesford.

This view looks along the towpath on top of the aqueduct towards Dowley Gap Mill, which was built as a worsted mill by Matthew and Thomas Walker in 1818.

Changeline bridge at Dowley Gap, *c*.1914. Here the towpath switches from the north bank to the south bank allowing the boatman and his horse to change sides and keep going in the same direction. Note the rectangular walled enclosure close to the bridge – this is a 'catchpit' to prevent pathway silt from Primrose Lane from spilling into the canal. A Canal Carrier boat has unloaded at the mill.

Dowley Gap Locks *c*.1930. The lock at Hirst Wood and these two rise locks commence a climb for the canal through Bingley of over 120ft. To the right is the lock-keeper's cottage and in the distance Hirst Woods and Shipley Glen.

Britannia Mill, Bingley, *c.*1930. A view over Bingley from Dubb Bridge, one of three crossings of the canal in Bingley. This small Yorkshire market town was transformed into an industrial community after 1759, firstly by the burning of local limestone and later by the worsted manufacture. Five mill chimneys and the spire of Mornington Road Church break the skyline here.

Three Rise Locks, *c.*1890. Several kilns for burning limestone were located to the right of this picture, in Lime Street. The kilns were probably built close to the canal wharves but both now lie buried beneath the premises of Bowling Green Mill (now Damart) in the top right of the photograph. Alongside are the Bingley Three Rise Locks (1774) built on the same staircase principle as their better known counterparts half a mile west of here. In the foreground is the old Bingley Railway Station, which closed in 1892.

Three Rise Locks, Bingley. Repairs to the lock gates are under way, *c.*1920.

Three Rise Locks. Joe Salt, a well-known Airedale boatman, prepares to take *Alpha* of the Skipton Co-operative Society through the locks as his horse is led up the tow path towards the lock-keeper's cottage.

Five Rise Locks, Bingley. One of the wonders of the early industrial world (there are bigger ones in France and Ireland) this staircase of five locks raises the canal 60ft and each lock holds between 80,000 and 90,000 gallons of water when full. The locks were designed by John Longbotham and the construction work was done by Barnabus Morvill, Jonathan Farrar and William Wild, all of Bingley. Much of the stonework was cut by John Sugden, a quarry owner from nearby Wilsden.

Five Rise Locks, Bingley, 1906. When they opened in March 1774, the first boat down (carrying coal) took twenty-eight minutes. The event was welcomed in Bingley by 'the ringing of church bells, a band of music, the firing of guns by the neighbouring Militia and the shouts of the spectators.' To the left in this picture is the carpenter's shop and, far right, a new swing bridge is being prepared.

Top Lock, Bingley Five Rise. In the centre of the photograph are the company stables where towing horses were fed and rested. The lock house close by was built in 1885 from a dismantled Liverpool warehouse; the building was brought, stone by stone, in barges along the canal.

The *Alexandra* at Bingley, *c.*1900. Jackets off and time to relax after climbing Bingley's staircase of five locks. A long straight and level stretch of canal allows these Victorian gentlemen to rest aboard this elegant steam-powered pleasure launch as it passes Gawthorpe Hall, an Elizabethan manor house, and its falconry.

Lime Kilns at Riddlesden. These kilns for burning raw limestone were located alongside, but below the level of, the canal (far right) at Riddlesden where Thomas Leach, as early as 1774, was burning lime and carrying it into the growing industrial town of Bradford.

Riddlesden, c.1904. This view is taken from the entrance to East Riddlesden Hall. In the centre of the picture, Granby Lane runs over the canal towards a small coal staithe and wharf alongside the bridge. At the time of this photograph they belonged to William Oldfield, canal carrier and coal merchant. The lime kilns and yard of the previous picture are to the rear of the small building on the right.

Marquis of Granby Inn, Riddlesden, c.1880. This public house was probably built at the same time as the canal (1774) which runs in front of it. From the small wharf here (centre), William Oldfield (1821-1898) added a carrying business to the coal trade inherited from his father. The photograph was taken on the occasion of the local fête known as 'Fanny's Fair'.

W. Oldfield Boat, 1998. The Oldfields continue to trade as coal merchants and lime burners but not, of course, from this modern pleasure narrow boat.

THE 'MARQUIS OF GRANBY'. RIDDLESDEN.   10575

Another view of the Marquis of Granby and Oldfield's Wharf from the towpath on the other side of the canal bridge.

Stockbridge. In 1821, there was an abortive attempt to link Keighley to the Leeds & Liverpool Canal by means of a branch canal from Utley which included eleven road bridges and a twelve arch aqueduct over the river. The estimated cost of £31,455 proved prohibitive and the town had to settle for the wharfage and warehousing at Stockbridge, seen here in the depths of the winter of 1996.

Leach's Bridge, 1926. The Morton Bus Company's fleet of three buses of French design brought the villagers of East and West Morton into the valley towns of Keighley and Bingley in the inter-war years.

Riddlesden, c.1912. The green fields running down to the canalside gave way to Keighley's urban sprawl about this time. These superior detached properties on Scott Lane came with their own private boathouse on the canalside, further encouraging the shift in the canal's use from commerce to leisure.

The Canal at Keighley, summer 1941, the canal between Riddlesden and Utley. The lane in the centre of the picture leads to Peck Wood and Willow Bank. The cottage in the distance was the home of a well-known muffin maker.

Willow Bank, Keighley. Running repairs to a minor canal breach at Willow Bank in 1955.

Keighley Golf Club, 1952. A much more serious breach of the canal on the stretch between Keighley and Silsden. The golf club lost two holes and the Leeds & Liverpool Canal Company lost millions of gallons of water.

Two

The Route (ii)

Keeping to the broad valley bottom the course of the Leeds & Liverpool Canal now leads westwards from Keighley towards Kildwick, affording excellent open views across the Aire Valley towards Crosshills. At Kildwick we have travelled approximately twenty-five miles from the centre of Leeds. Skirting round the pretty Pennine village of Farnhill, the canal heads north past Farnhill Wood with marvellous views across the valley, to the lead-mining village of Cononley. The canal then loops westwards towards Bradley before continuing its twisting way into the ancient town of Skipton.

During the twentieth century pleasure cruising along the canal became increasingly popular at several points on the eastern side of the Pennines (Bingley, Shipley, Rodley, etc.). No more so than at Skipton, where the canal is joined by a small eighteenth-century branch canal (Springs Canal) linking limestone quarries at Eller Beck, at the rear of Skipton Castle. Heading north-eastward, the canal passes the infrastructure of Skipton's industrial revolution, including old textile factories, millworkers' housing, warehouses and wharves, before breaking out once more into open pasture lands where the canal travels beneath the Skipton bypass road of the A59. Road and canal pass close together at Thorlby swing bridge before the canal bears westward close to the A65 road on its way to the old cotton village of Gargrave. There, the canal keeps to the northern boundary of the village, which enjoyed increased commercial prosperity in the last quarter of the eighteenth century when it became for a short time the western terminus of the Yorkshire section of the canal.

Work on the Yorkshire side of the canal stopped here in March 1774 and did not begin again until October 1790. It was important for the company to reach this point at Eshton Road Bridge as the main water supply for the Yorkshire stretch of the canal was from Eshton Beck.

Leaving Gargrave via a series of six locks, the line of the canal now heads westwards towards the Aire Gap and crosses the River Aire once more at Priestholme Bridge on a well proportioned aqueduct 400ft above mean sea level. At Bank Newton, the canal journeys once again through a series of six locks which lift the canal another 50ft. The canal basin at the top of the locks hosts the former Canal Company's workshops, now a busy marina and boat hire centre. The storehouse in the carpenter's yard at Bank Newton housed all the Leeds & Liverpool Company's legal records during the Second World War.

From there the line of the canal meanders in a series of twisting loops using the natural contours of the terrain to make its way to East Marton, famous for its double arched bridge over the canal. The canal is now approaching the county border with Lancashire and is surrounded on both sides by some striking Pennine landscape of grassy hillocks (glacial drumlins). The towpath goes under Old Hall and South Field bridges and eventually reaches Greenberfield Changeline Bridge. At Greenberfield, the original three lock staircase was replaced, as early as 1820, by three separate locks in order to save water. Traces of the original line of the canal can be spotted by a discerning eye. At Greenberfield we are forty one miles from Leeds and the locks there raise the canal to its summit pound, 487ft above sea level. The feeder pipeline from Winterburn Reservoir (nine miles away) enters the summit pound at this point. To ensure a water supply to the canal, this reservoir (holding 280 million gallons of water) was built in 1892. From here the canal moves in the direction of Barnoldswick ('Barlick') and there the coverage of the canal in this publication ends.

Keighley district. From Bingley Five Rise the canal continues westwards as a level lock-free pound, bypassing the industrial town of Keighley as it does so. There follows a long, straight stretch of canal to Silsden. Hugging the hillside on an elevated position above the valley, the canal affords some spectacular long open views across Airedale's glacial lake flats at this point.

A company maintenance boat at Silsden Aqueduct, 1954.

Silsden, c.1900. The Silsden Co-operative coal boat *Progress* iced-up, with Earl Dawson and Silas Clarke aboard.

Kildwick, 1890. Peter Baldwin aboard the short boat *Five Rise* in the long hot summer of 1890. This was a boat used by the company's carpenters for site repair work.

Apollo Canal Transport's boat *Wye* about to approach Shipton in April 1973. This diesel-powered short boat, built in 1947, is loaded with coal and bound for Laycock's and the Embsay Railway. Aboard are David Lowe, Joe Bridge and John Cheetham.

Thornton's Staith, c.1960. Having passed through some typical Pennine countryside of old mill villages, open moorland and sweeping green valley locations, the canal bypasses Farnhill, Snaygill and Bradley to approach the old market town of Skipton. Here at Thornton's Staith is another Gallows Bridge (after a hanging gallows, i.e. with a staircase at each end) originally wooden but replaced in 1974 by a steel structure. In the distance is the chimney to Fell's leadworks and extreme right is the blocked up loading bay to Skipton gasworks. To the left is the yard and office of P. Thornton, an early carrier on the canal.

'Tin Bridge', Skipton, *c*.1960, a footbridge over the canal between Sackville Street (right) and Lower Union Street (left). It was built during the First World War to allow workers access to the munitions factory nearby. Former loading bays have been blocked up in the wall adjoining the canal. The mill is now demolished.

Pinder Bridge, Skipton, *c*.1975. A narrow boat passes beneath the bridge (Keighley Road) and moves alongside Pethybridge's Warehouse (right). To the left is the bus station at Skipton.

Belmont Bridge, Skipton, 1928. This bridge over the Leeds & Liverpool Canal is located shortly before the junction with the Springs Canal (to the left) at the Skipton basin. The *Alpha* is one of the boats moored beside the original eighteenth century warehouse of the company. In the centre are Winterwell Buildings built in 1889, and to the right are the ancient premises of carpenter Thomas Duckett.

Skipton Wharf, 1925. Unloading the steamer *Beta*, a B.C. Walls boat, at Skipton in 1925. Alongside is the motor boat *Kappa*. Both are discharging their cargoes into the original eighteenth century warehousing of the Canal Company.

Springs Canal Junction, *c.*1960. At the Skipton basin this branch canal links into the Leeds & Liverpool Canal to follow a route past the church and behind Skipton Castle to the limestone waggon way from the Haw Park quarries of the Earl of Thanet (1785).

Flyboats at Skipton, *c.*1930. Canal Transport Company flyboats possibly loaded with baled wool and ready to leave Skipton basin. Tarpaulin covers protected the cargo from bad weather. Later boats carrying grain had covered hatches.

Quiet water, Niffany Farm, *c.*1960. An almost perfect symmetry in the reflection of the landscape in the canal. At the swing bridge at Niffany Farm (right) the towpath becomes part of the pavement of the A629. Here, goods were once transhipped to the London & North Western Railway.

Gargrave, *c.*1930. Replacing the old arch bridge with a new structure at Gargrave in the 1930s. Short boat *Annie* serves as the maintenance boat. Bowler hats and trilbys mean you look on; flat caps denote hard graft.

Green's Mill, Gargrave, c.1900. Semi-loaded flyboats here at Gargrave would suggest a drought and the canal was too shallow for movement. By 1900 Mr Green of Gargrave had opened a coal yard beyond the bridge close to the lock. In 1998 the premises were still selling domestic coal from the Prince of Wales Colliery, Pontefract. The mill was also a flour mill and close by was the wharf which received lead from the mines at Grassington.

No.3 Lock, Gargrave, c.1900. Beneath the bridge is one of Gargrave's six locks. To the left the lock-keeper's cottage is undergoing extension work. The white vertical line on the bridge arch marked the centre of the navigable channel and was particularly useful for night-time navigation or winter mornings.

Higherland Lock, *c.1958*. At Higherland Bridge, the Pennine Way crosses the canal. Here, at nearby Higherland Lock House in 1843, Benjamin Walls was employed by the Canal Company as supervisor of the water supply to the Skipton Pool, i.e. the stretch between Gargrave and Bingley. Eight children were born here to Walls and his second wife, including Benjamin Curry Walls, who became a canal employee at sixteen in 1893. He later moved to Belle Vue Terrace, Skipton, moving all his belongings from door to door by canal barge.

Gargrave. The short boat *Crucis* approaches Gargrave where the canal follows the Aire Gap, the lowest point for crossing the Pennines.

Bank Newton, *c.*1892. Thirty-six miles from the Leeds basin is the maintenance yard at Bank Newton. The conduit pipes stacked in the yard were to be used for a new pipeline to take water from Winterburn Reservoir to the canal at Greenberfield in 1892.

Bottom Lock, Bank Newton. 1892 again if the solitary cow is the same one as in the previous photograph! Here, company maintenance boats were built. The building to the right is the lock-keeper's cottage.

Bank Newton, 1954. This is the fourth of six locks at Newton Grange which raise the canal 50ft in total. At the tail of lock six we are 400ft above mean sea level. At the top of the locks there are stunning panoramic views across Craven and Flasby Fell.

Bank Newton, c.1960. The carpenter's yard again in the early 1960s. Today the yard and premises serve as a marina and a busy boat-hire centre.

East Marton, 1896. From Bank Newton the canal takes a series of twisting loops, leaving behind the Aire Gap for East Marton and its famous double arched bridge which carries the busy A59 Skipton to Clitheroe road over the canal. The bridge is thought to have been built at the same time as the canal in 1772, when engineers did not bother to level roads. As the science of road building improved, roads were levelled off and a second bridge was added, acting as a buttress to the first... probably.

Ice-breaking at East Marton, c.1939. The 'V' shaped boat was rocked violently from side to side by company employees and towed by as many as a dozen horses. Here at East Marton two animals seem to be sufficient for the job in hand.

Greenberfield, c.1930. Once beyond East and West Marton the canal travels through some typical Craven countryside (top right) of grassy hillocks or drumlins, which give a rolling atmosphere to the landscape. As the canal twists round Risebrigg Hill, the county boundary is crossed and Greenberfield is in view. Here, a traditional flyboat is horse-towed by a typical crew of two to three men.

Greenberfield Locks, c.1920. The first boats went through in 1816 when the canal was completed. This is the highest point on the canal, 487ft above mean sea level. Water is supplied by a pipe from Winterburn Reservoir, nine miles away. This photograph shows the re-routed canal. The original line went through a three lock staircase but this consumed too much water and often flooded so the canal was re-routed through three separate locks in 1828 on the advice of John Rennie, who also recommended the removal of Bingley Five Rise in favour of a series of single locks. To the relief of Bradford Metropolitan District Council's tourist committee, this was not acted upon.

Top Lock, Greenberfield. A flyboat in the top lock at Greenberfield. From here, the canal follows the natural contours, skirting round the workshops of Rolls-Royce Aerospace and avoiding the centre of Barnoldswick, with its branch canal to Rain Hall limestone quarry.

Foulridge Tunnel, Eastern End. Once round the village of Salterforth, the canal cuts through open pasture lands and at Foulridge enters a lengthy tunnel (1,640 yards). Before the introduction of the steam tug, barges were 'walked' through by means of professional 'leggers' who laid on their backs and pushed their feet against the wall of the tunnel. The tow horse meanwhile was led over the hill by the bargee. From 1880 a steam tug was provided at Foulridge to tow boats through the tunnel at a loaded charge of 5/- per boat and light charge of 2/6. Some boatmen continued to leg their boats through while still claiming the towage fee. The tug was double-ended with a propeller and rudder at each end to save time. The service ended when most boats had their own engines. The last boat towed through to Yorkshire was the *Bison* in March 1937. Note the keystone over the tunnel entrance showing the completion year of the tunnel, 1792.

Three
Branch Canals

It was always the intention of the original promoters of the Leeds & Liverpool Canal to build branch lines connecting individual towns and industries. On the eastern side of the Pennines the most important of these was the Bradford Canal, which was built simultaneously with the main canal in 1774. Elsewhere I have argued that this was the catalyst to the major scheme from the very outset i.e. the movement of Bradford coal into Craven in exchange for Skipton limestone for burning into lime. The canal's definitive history by Mike Clarke has rightly argued that limestone, eventually, was not the major trade along the line as early as 1800 but in 1770 its importance must not be underestimated to the dozen or so Bradford colliery owners, headed by John Hustler and Abraham Balme. They were selling coal in the Skipton area and bringing back into an expanding Bradford, burnt lime for building, iron smelting and land improvement.

The Bradford Canal

With the passing of the Leeds & Liverpool Act in 1770 the cabal of Bradford colliery owners quickly obtained (April 1771) an Act for a canal of three and a half miles with ten locks on the stretch between the centre of Bradford and the junction with the Leeds & Liverpool scheme at Windhill, Shipley. Twenty-eight subscribers donated £6,000 for the cost of the canal which opened in September 1774 when Abraham Balme's boat, the *Good Intent* was despatched to Bingley with a load of coal. The Bradford Lime Kiln Company quickly established lime burning kilns alongside the canal, close to the centre of the town. Water supply to the Bradford Canal was a problem from the outset and when dozens of textile mills suddenly appeared after 1800, the competition for water grew even fiercer. As early as 1825 traders in the town complained of the slow boat journey from Shipley: three days for four miles. By 1849 the water in the canal was so polluted that a cholera epidemic in the area of the canal caused over 400 deaths, leading to harsh criticism from a government health official and a demand for closure by the townspeople. The opening of the Leeds-Bradford railway in 1846 signalled the end of the canal's commercial viability and in 1864 the Bradford Canal Company was taken to court for use of impure water and creating a public health hazard. One witness said:

> As to the Bradford Canal I have only to remark that it is a life-destroying monster nuisance... It is a literal fact that it has been on fire. A light fell accidentally overboard from one of the boats and the matter which composes the canal actually ignited.

Little wonder the canal was closed in 1866 and the last quarter of a mile was filled in. The Leeds & Liverpool Company offered to lease the canal and pump in water from their own supplies. Consequently the canal was re-opened in 1872, beginning at Northbrook Bridge with wharves in Wharf Street and Canal Street. Five pump houses were built to pump water from one lock to the next at a cost of £8 per annum per boat. Consequently the company showed little profit and by 1922 was losing over £3,500 per year. On 15 July that year, the last boat, the *Beta*, navigated the canal and the waterway was closed forever.

Springs Canal, Skipton

This was another branch canal conceived early in the scheme for the Leeds & Liverpool Canal. Lord Thanet, who owned rich mineral estates around Skipton, had opposed the Aire & Calder Navigation in 1744 but his successor could see the potential of a canal to his limestone quarries behind Skipton Castle. The Act for the Springs Canal was passed in 1773 and was completed a year later owing to its quarter of a mile length. From 1785 the Canal Company took over the lease of the quarries and held it well into the nineteenth century, delivering limestone via chutes and staithes and a waggonway into boats beneath the castle.

Rain Hall Quarry, Barnoldswick

In January 1796 the company devised a branch canal to Rain Hall Rock limestone quarry near Barnoldswick. The canal was built through two tunnels directly into the limestone outcrop. Eventually as the limestone was worked out, the branch canal was about 600 yards long when the quarry closed in the 1890s.

There were several abortive branch canals to Selby, Settle and Keighley which never reached the statute book.

Settle Canal

It was the intention of the original scheme to build a branch canal to Settle but the traders and merchants of the town insisted upon an entirely separate scheme and in 1774 they petitioned Parliament for a fifteen-mile-long canal. This, however, was strongly opposed by local landowners and the scheme was dropped, only to be resurrected in 1780 with a complicated canal link between Settle and Ingleton via Burton-in-Lonsdale and no fewer than forty-five locks down to the Ribble. The scheme was too ambitious for such a sparsely populated area and was dropped.

Keighley Canal

In 1821 the Yorkshire contingent on the Canal Company board of directors proposed a branch canal from the main waterway at Utley, to Keighley. This included a twelve arch aqueduct over the River Aire and a half mile embankment costing £31,455. The principal gentlemen, traders, manufacturers and Keighley inhabitants found this expense prohibitive and settled for the wharfage at Stockbridge and the scheme was never mentioned again.

Leeds and Selby Canal

At the time of the original Leeds & Liverpool Canal scheme there was considerable debate about the condition of the Aire & Calder Navigation into which the canal linked at Leeds. In place of improvements to the Navigation, John Longbotham proposed an entirely new canal from Leeds to Selby, via Methley. The proposal included four sets of staircase locks (two three-rise and two two-rise), twenty-three miles of cut and a 400 yard tunnel at Fairburn. The Bill for this canal was lost in 1774 because of an inadequate water supply but the estimated cost of £60,000 also proved prohibitive.

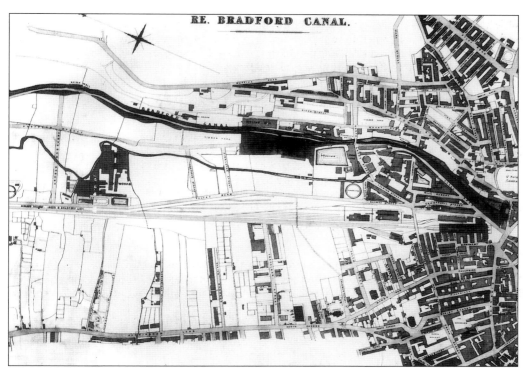

RE. BRADFORD CANAL.

Bradford Canal. Extract from an early plan of the Bradford Canal showing the line of the canal running into the very heart of the town below St Peter's Church.

Canal Basin, Bradford, c.1840. The stench and filth of this part of Bradford made it a public health hazard by 1845 when James Smith, a government inspector, described it as

> …So charged with decaying matter that in hot weather bubbles of sulphurated hydrogen are continually rising to the surface and so much is the atmosphere loaded with that gas, that watch cases and other materials of silver, become black in the pockets of workmen employed near the canal.

Spinkwell Locks *c.*1885, the first of ten locks leaving the centre of Bradford. By the time of this photograph the line of the canal had been truncated and its new terminus was not too far to the left of this picture. The building in the right foreground was one of several engine houses for pumping water into the canal.

Spinkwell Lock gates, 1969. Built at the canal's highest point, Spinkwell was a popular picnic spot in the late nineteenth century and was the last of the canal's locks to close. it was in a poor state of repair in 1969 and was finally demolished in March 1995 to make way for industrial units and road development.

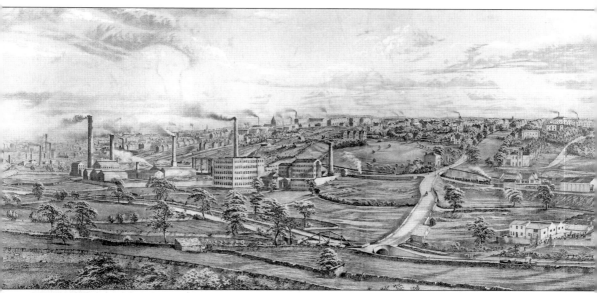

Bradford from the north-east. The Bradford Canal sweeps majestically through the green fields and suburbs of Bolton and Manningham. This stretch of the canal is between Spinkwell Locks (far left) and Oliver Locks.

Line of the Bradford Canal at Bolton Woods, looking towards Oliver Locks which lowered the canal 18ft.

Windhill Locks, Bradford Canal *c.*1955. Used as a location for the film *Room at the Top*.

Windhill Bridge, *c.*1880. On this occasion the arched stone canal bridge of 1774 was replaced by a wider metal structure.

Pumping station, Dock Lane, Windhill *c.*1952. With the formation of a new company in 1871 the Bradford Canal's chronic water supply was partially resolved by drawing water from the main canal at Shipley by means of steam-driven pumps. There were several of these pumping stations along the line of the branch canal. This one at Dock Lane began the process.

Bradford Canal closure, 1922. Ben Wall's boat *Beta* was the last barge to take cargo on the canal in 1922. Here, it is seen leaving Northbrook Bridge (the new terminus of 1871) in the direction of Shipley.

Springs Canal, Skipton, 1928. The canal basin at Skipton where the Springs Canal joins with the Leeds & Liverpool. In the foreground is a traditional Leeds & Liverpool Canal barge with the squared chimney typical of boats on the east of the Pennines. To the left is Coach Street Bridge.

Springs Canal, c.1930. Beyond Coach Street Bridge, the short arm of the canal stretches alongside the narrow channel of Eller Beck towards Skipton Castle, beyond the Parish Church.

Water Street, Skipton, formerly boatmen's homes and lodging houses.

Springs Canal, Mill Bridge, *c.*1960. The canal as it approaches Mill Bridge, Skipton. In the background are the premises of two well-known boating inns, the Ship Inn on the left and the Castle Inn on the right.

High Corn Mill, Springs Canal, c.1960. In 1954 Skipton Castle Estates sold their properties and George Leatt purchased Skipton's old corn mill above Mill Bridge. The mill, powered by a huge water wheel, was later converted into a folk museum and more recently has converted to shops and offices. The Springs Canal runs here alongside the old mill and bends to the right at the rear of Skipton Castle.

Springs Canal, 1955. A metal dredger and maintenance boat are ice bound at the rear of the castle in 1955. In the distance can be seen the old chutes which dropped limestone from the Haw Bank Quarry tramway into awaiting barges beneath the castle escarpment.

Four

Boats on the Canal

When the Leeds & Liverpool Canal was conceived in the 1760s, keel boats (60ft long and 14ft wide) were already in service on the Aire & Calder Navigation which flowed into the tidal estuary of the River Humber. As the canal was initially planned and promoted on the eastern side of the Pennines and approved by Robert Whitworth, it was natural for many of the early boats to match this style and these dimensions (as do the lock sizes).

Early barges in Yorkshire evolved from the coastal trading vessel, the Yorkshire keelboat, which was 'clinker-built' (where planks were overlapped and riveted to make them watertight). By contrast, boats which worked below Wigan, between Leigh and Liverpool, were 73ft in length and slightly broader in the beam. Lancashire boats tended to be built of carvel construction where the planks were adjacent to each other and caulked with oakum to make them watertight.

VESSELS FOR SALE.

To be Sold by Auction,

AT TWO O'CLOCK IN THE AFTERNOON, OF

Friday, the 16th Day of May 1834,

AT THE BASIN OR WHARF,

Of the Leeds and Liverpool Canal, at SKIPTON, in the County of York;

2 GOOD STRONG Vessels,

CLINKER BUILT.

Known by the names of the JUNCTION and the INDUSTRY, registering about 40 Tons each.

The Junction has only been built about 9 or 10 Years.

The VESSELS may be seen near the Tonnage Bridge in Skipton, until the Day of Sale.

Further Particulars may be had of

Mr. Alcock, Solicitor,

SKIPTON.

J. GARNETT, Printer, Bookseller, Bookbinder, and Stationer, Skipton.

In this advertisement of 1834, two Yorkshire short boats are up for sale at the Skipton basin. Mike Clarke tells us that 'clinker-built' boats died out in the 1850s as a result of their susceptibility to damage at the locks and at bridges.

Isabella at Skipton Basin. A typical Yorkshire short boat loading with general merchandise at the original canal company warehouse at Skipton, occupied by Ben C. Walls & Co. when this photograph was taken. As the boatman fastens down protective sheets, his children play at the stern of the boat.

Stuck! Here, Master Harry Peet has wedged his wide boat in Wigan Lock in 1939, involving the company in considerable expense and inconvenience.

Edith at Bingley Five Rise Locks, *c*.1930. This typical square-sterned coal barge is probably in tow of the steamer ahead. The usual deck furniture aboard the *Edith* can be seen: water barrel, horse provender box and stern rails, only the dog kennel is missing here. J.R. Thornton was a Skipton carrier.

Lizzie – another square-sterned barge belonging to Robert Foster of Shipley and built at Ramsey's boatyard in the town. The square, panelled stern provided boat painters with greater potential for their skills.

Armley, a maintenance boat of the Canal Transport Company, is beached after the canal had burst its bank at Peck Wood, Riddlesden, in 1952.

Bradford, a 'town' class short boat built in the early 1950s, at Burscough c.1949.

Company boatyard, Finsley Gate, Burnley. Here also was the company sawmill for the whole length of the canal. Boats were made or repaired here on stocks and then launched sideways into the canal. Maintenance boats were also built at the company's yards at Bank Newton and Apperley Bridge.

Steam-driven short boat, Skipton c.1950. Steam power was first introduced on the Yorkshire stretch of the canal in 1866 when the Airedale Tug Company towed horse boats on the river between Leeds Bridge and the first canal lock. Steam-driven boats on the whole line of the canal became a common sight after 1880, although horses were used for haulage well into the 1950s. Here Bill Hesketh steers a cargo of domestic coal for J.R. Thornton of Skipton. The nautical fellow is said to be Tom Barrett.

The steam flyboats *Beaver*, *Agate*, and *Amy*, ice-bound at the top of Five Rise Locks, Bingley, c.1915.

Another Thornton boat, *Walter*, passes a swing bridge at Skipton. This old horse-drawn boat had a 1930s engine adapted to it.

Flyboats at Gargrave, c.1900. From 1880, the company introduced steam-powered, cargo-carrying flyboats which towed three or four 'dumb' (unpowered) boats and used horses for towing through locks. Here, several company flyboats are tied up at Gargrave, c.1900, possibly due to drought conditions or repair work ahead.

H. Widdop & Co. Ltd of Keighley became the best-known supplier of diesel engines on the Yorkshire side of the canal. Diesel power had been tried as early as 1903 and was popular with Benjamin Wall's company after 1924.

Capella at Hirst Wood, Shipley, 1938. This diesel-powered general merchandise boat travels on the picturesque stretch of the canal between Hirst Lock and the Dowley Gap Locks.

Up to a dozen horses pulled this old company ice-breaking boat which was triangular in section. Horse ropes were attached to the short masts and ropes from the larger masts were swayed alternately by the boatmen, forcing ice to break as far as both banks. Ballast in the stern tilted the boat's iron clad bow out of the water to enable it to come crashing down on ice in front. Wooden ridges on the sides of the boat prevented lateral damage.

An iron dredger, Skipton Basin, 1947. Iron boats were first purchased by the company in 1875 but they were expensive and not popular with the boatmen who found them uncomfortable. No more iron barges were purchased until motor boats were built for Canal Transport in 1932. However, iron was favoured for steam-powered dredging boats like this one at Skipton in 1947. Coach Street Bridge and Skipton Parish Church are visible in the background.

The early spoon dredger *Sir Robert* at Kildwick. The man on the left is manually working the crane to lower and raise the spoon, which was filled with rubbish as it scraped the bed of the canal. It was then emptied into the boat by the man on the right.

A huge iron dredging hopper is launched at the Apperley Bridge maintenance yard in 1955. The boat had travelled from Distingo, in Cumbria.

Water Witch, Bingley. One of the Leeds & Liverpool Company's small fleet of steam-driven cabin cruisers, the *Water Witch* carried directors and important customers along the Bingley-Skipton stretch of the canal. Here, the boat is moored at the top of the Five Rise Locks. This elegant vessel was used at the opening of Winterburn Reservoir in 1893 and was still in company use in 1945.

Victoria, another company cruiser reserved for company officials and engineering surveys, is seen here tied up at Kildwick.

Alexandra was another of the company's fleet of elegant steam launches, used by directors largely on the Yorkshire side of the Pennines. Here it is moored at Buck Woods, Thackley.

The launch of the *Rocine* at Shipley. This pleasure launch is about to take to the water at Dockfields swing bridge, near Shipley, in 1920. In the background, on the right, a commercial barge is also ready for launching broadside into the canal. Pleasure boating on the Yorkshire side of the canal was particularly popular in the Victorian era at Skipton and Saltaire, until government regulations reduced unlicensed boats to only twelve passengers.

Ramsey's boatyard, Junction Dock, Shipley. G.E. Ramsey's boatyard was one of over thirty such yards on the canal and, although a private concern, was used by the Leeds & Liverpool Company for the construction and repair of its carrying fleet. The large timber store and sawmill can be seen to the left in the background. to the fore, is a new Ramsey motorized coal boat with heightened bow cabin.

Five
Repairs and Maintenance

The original work of cutting the canal was essentially a manual task carried out by a breed of tough, hard-working and hard-living men, many of whom came from Ireland and Scotland or from the more remote dales of Yorkshire. Digging and puddling the original canal was hard and dirty work for the navigators ('navvies'), who were often exploited by country innkeepers for their food and accommodation. The Company was therefore forced to provide houses and provisions for their cutters.

Much of the original labour was put out under contract to local companies along the route who were responsible for hiring a vast army of brick-makers, stonemasons, carpenters and engineers. Their equipment was basically the spade, shovel, pick, bucket and wheelbarrow. Some of these men were fortunate to find permanent employment with the Leeds & Liverpool Company when the canal was completed in 1816.

Subsequent canal maintenance and repair work can be divided into three distinct categories. Most important was the maintenance of the canal's correct water level. Secondly, was the upkeep of canal banks and bridges. Lastly, was the preservation of locks. In this section of the book we shall look at these three in reverse order.

Company Maintenance Boat, Salterforth. Here, banksmen relax at Salterforth cottages aboard the company houseboat No.2 when undertaking work away from their depot and their homes.

Repair Team, East Marton 1902. This group of men were responsible for the maintenance of the canal on the Yorkshire side from Greenberfield to Leeds at the turn of the century. They were led by Benjamin Walls (far right), who was promoted to Company Traffic Inspector the following year. They appear too well-dressed for work and were probably on a works trip to Marton aboard a company launch.

John Bishop of Skipton. A holder of many jobs and offices in the service of the Leeds & Liverpool Canal Company and later in the employ of B.C. Walls. He worked for many years in the engineers' workshop at Skipton Basin. He was mate aboard the steam cruiser *Alexandra* and general odd-job man into his eighties. He is seen here at the tiller of the *Alexandra*.

New Lock Gate, Bingley, c.1895. A new lock gate has just been delivered at Bingley's Five Rise and is being lifted into place by sheer legs. To the right, a new swing bridge is also ready for the top of the locks.

Tea Break. The same scene with the tail gate suspended (supported by the boat) until the gentleman on the ladder has finished his 'drinking'. New sills for the canalside lie on the towpath and in the distance is Bingley's Bowling Green Mill, site of the Three Rise Locks.

Bingley Five Rise, c.1895. A dramatic photograph from inside the fully drained staircase locks of Bingley Five Rise. The three gentlemen in front are repairing the sill at the bottom of the lock which sealed it when closed.

The new swing bridge at Bingley, c.1895. Draining the canal in preparation for the bridge's installation required the insertion of several stop planks by means of the hand powered pile driver (right). The piled stone on the left is ready for the building of a new stable block.

Finsley Gate, Burnley, 1907. Huge amounts of timber were worked at the Company's boatyards at Apperley Bridge and Burnley's Finsley Gate. This steam-powered saw at Burnley replaced the old manual method of a sawpit.

The carpenter's yard, 1936. On the Yorkshire side of the canal much of the repair work was done at the carpenter's yard at Apperley Bridge. Here, in 1936, Tom Pemberton uses a range of old tools to fashion a new balance beam.

Repairs to the canal bank, Bingley. Repairing sills and bridges along the canal was the second major category of maintenance work and here, at the bottom of Five Rise Locks, Noah Banks is awaiting a delivery of cement for repair work on the sills of the lock and the canalside.

Bridge repairs, Bingley, 1973. The maintenance of road bridges was originally the Company's responsibility but with increased traffic in Yorkshire's rapidly growing towns, the duty of repair eventually became a shared one. Here at Bingley, Dubb Bridge, an original bridge, is replaced by a more modern structure in 1973.

Storm damage at Springs Canal, Skipton. Sustaining the water level in the canal was largely the work of those who supervised the company's reservoirs but occasionally the water level was affected by other factors. Here, storm damage has enforced the drainage of the Springs Canal until the repair work is completed. Mid-twentieth century and the work is still very manual with pick, shovel and wheelbarrow and plenty of honest Yorkshire graft.

Ice-breaking, Farnhill, 1939. Ice was a perennial problem for the canal company and could hold up traffic for long periods. Here at Farnhill Woods near Skipton in the winter of 1939-1940 the boat seems to be in difficulty.

In fact the V-shaped boat (made from oak with a steel prow) was deliberately rocked from side to side by as many as six men.

Ice-breaking at the Farnhill-Skipton stretch, 1940. When the ice was too thick, the boat could often slither on the surface of the canal.

A company boat often followed the ice-breaker to crush the ice into still smaller pieces and make the canal passable once more. John Draper and Herbert Greenwood are doing exactly that.

Ice-breaking, c.1950. By the time this photograph was taken, more powerful equipment was used for breaking the ice. This specially equipped steam tug seems to be having the right effect.

Apperley Bridge, c.1955. After the Second World War, much of the maintenance of the canal on the Yorkshire side was centred at the carpenter's yard at Apperley Bridge. Here, a new culvert is being laid not far from the old boatyard (on the right in the background.

Lock repair at Apperley Bridge, 1950s. A hand-operated pile driver knocks in stop planks. Originally the floors of the locks were wooden and later reinforced with concrete.

Lock repairs, Apperley, 1950s. This wheelbarrow ramp would offend modern health and safety policies.

Deep lock diving, Apperley Bridge. A diver is needed to inspect the walls of the lock and the ground paddles (openings for filling and emptying the locks). Stanley Wade here assists with the ladder.

Keighley, breach repairs, 1952. Spoon dredger on maintenance boat at Keighley Golf course.

Flood damage at Skipton, 1908. Quarry tramway wagons are used to clear debris in the Springs Canal.

Six

Historical Developments After 1820

Once completed, the Leeds & Liverpool Canal was an immediate financial success. Although the predicted trade in limestone did not materialize, it was more than compensated for by the huge profits in general merchandise which commanded a much higher tollage than either limestone or coal. Coal tonnage from coalfields in both Yorkshire and Lancashire soared to two and a half millions tons. By 1824 the line earned profits of £94,423 allowing a share dividend of £15. By 1840 this dividend was doubled allowing the company to pay off all of its debts.

In order to compete with the new railways (the Leeds-Manchester railway was opened in 1836 and the Leeds-Bradford line followed a decade later) the Canal Company continued to improve its waterway facilities. As competition with the railways sharpened, canal profits slumped, particularly in the merchandise sector which ranged from food, textiles and alcohol, to gunpowder and manure. However, competition also affected railway profits and, in 1850, a deal was struck between the Canal Company and the railways leasing all merchandise tolls to the trains for £31,000 per annum for twenty-one years. This guaranteed an income to the company for a trade sector it was in danger of losing.

Initially, carrying goods along the canal was done by private carriers like William Oldfield, of Riddlesden, and the Canal Company did not involve itself in this aspect of business until the carriage rates from railway companies became too competitive for small individual carriers. The second Canal Carriers Act of 1847 allowed companies to borrow money to organize their own carrying departments. Consequently, in 1848, the Leeds & Liverpool Company purchased the boats of the major traders along the canal and commenced in the carrying business in its own right. The logistics of the mineral industries in northern England meant that the new railway companies were unable to compete effectively in coal and limestone. They settled instead for an unexpected monopoly of passenger carriage and an increased share of the general merchandise business.

By August 1874 the Canal Company was in a sufficiently strong financial position to take responsibility again for running the merchandise traffic on the canal. Healthy financial reserves enabled them to immediately undercut carriage rates of the railways whose service had become sloppy and inefficient. However, during the period of the railway lease much of the canal infrastructure had been neglected and there was an urgent need for improvements along the whole line of the canal in warehouse renewals, bridge rebuilding, water supply and, more importantly, in the number and quality of the aborted carrying fleet which had been reduced from eighty one boats to thirty during the lease period. By 1875 the Canal Company had built up its fleet of boats to sixty, although more than half the trade continued to be carried in bye-traders' boats. Another major investment in this period was the introduction of steam-powered cargo carrying flyboats. These were able to tow up to four unpowered flyboats (dumb boats) delivering a variety of cargoes on a regular and speedier timetable. This system also enabled the company to shift small cargoes shorter distances, further increasing competition with the railway companies.

By 1890 this advantage had been lost when the Railway and Canal Traffic Act of 1888 forced canal companies to bring their carriage rates in line with those of the railways, although this did not apply to the individual bye-traders on the canal. This disastrous piece of legislation coincided with a massive programme of capital investment by the company.

An Act of 1891 had restructured the company as the 'Leeds & Liverpool Canal Company' with an increased share issue of £275,000 for these improvements. The intention was to upgrade the canal to enable it to carry boats of sixty-seven tons. Dredgers and cranes were purchased for the Leeds end of the canal and almost £100,000 was spent on deepening the stretch of canal between Leeds and Shipley. Dividends dropped dramatically and shareholders in London questioned the wisdom of improvement schemes. In consequence, much of the improvement programme was diluted and the company's financial situation was desperate by the end of the century. Despite an increase in the volume of goods carried, there was a 30% decrease in income from tolls between 1890 and 1900. To add insult to injury, the weather in that decade did not help their cause. A hard winter in 1895 closed the whole canal for two months and there were summer droughts in six out of the ten years.

The company's financial situation was aggravated by the outbreak of war in 1914 when the canal was placed under a Board of Trade committee until 1920. Then the government subsidy ceased, immediately leaving the Canal Company in a desperate state. By 1921 the canal carrying company was all but bankrupt and a large number of boats were tied up for the lack of crews. This, and the carrying company's unstable financial situation, resulted in the closure of that part of the company's business activities.

Other assets of the Canal Company were gradually sold, including that of the Bradford Canal which was finally shut down in 1922. The coal demands of several power stations along the line of the canal, including Kirkstall and Whitehall Road, Leeds, brought a temporary respite. New wool warehouses were constructed at Stockbridge (Keighley) and at Shipley but the Canal Company was in a state of terminal decline. A few bye-traders like Benjamin C. Walls carried on the merchandise trade, particularly in sugar, cement and barley. Walls had a fleet of twenty boats named after letters of the Greek alphabet and he did good business in raw wool at Shipley and Keighley. By 1921 three main firms continued to carry general merchandise along the canal: John Hunt & Sons, Benjamin C. Walls and Lancashire Canal Transport, which, by 1929, was in serious financial difficulties. In the following year the Canal Company forced an amalgamation of the three by creating a new company, Canal Transport Ltd, in which the Leeds & Liverpool Company owned a 51% share.

In July 1929 the maintenance of the canal was rationalized, the canal being divided into four sections each with a general foreman. Fred Bateman became senior inspector for the stretch between Leeds and Blackburn. During the Second World War the canal was in frequent use to transport desperately needed cargoes. Women were trained to work the barges in the absence of men at war. Also, as visits to the seaside were limited, 'Holidays at Home' were planned and the canal became very popular for pleasure trips.

The Leeds & Liverpool Canal Company was fully nationalized in 1948. Thereafter little money was spent on the repair and maintenance of canal banks, lock gates, etc. Traditional coal powered factories along the canal turned to electricity; road transport became cheaper and the textile trades were chronically depressed. The great freeze of 1963, when the canal was closed for several weeks, was the final nail in the company's coffin. The last commercial delivery on the waterway was to the Liverpool Gas Works in 1973, almost 200 years after the first. In the 1968 Transport Act, the line was categorized as a pleasure cruising waterway.

Today, under the control of British Waterways, it is maintained for its amenity value to the community. With the way of the world at the end of the second millennium, leisure and recreation have replaced commerce and trade.

Seven

Boat Life

In the heyday of the canals boatmen were a fairly rough and brash lot. Families worked on the canal for several generations; particular families identifying with particular stretches of the canal: the Oldfields at Riddlesden, the Walls at Gargrave and the Holmes family at Shipley. The latter had a distinctive way of handling a boat which was easily recognized by other boatmen. A traditional crew was made up of the master and his mate. On 31 March 1881, the census enumerator found nine boats tied up at the Shipley Wharf. These were mostly made up of two-men crews but there were also some family boats such as the *James*, where Joe Duckworth was aboard with his eleven-year old adopted son, and the *Ada* which was inhabited by Captain Jonas Spencer, his unmarried partner and their baby daughter, Mary Elizabeth. Sometimes, on these boats, children acted as mates and thus reduced costs. Aboard the *Jupiter*, Henry Draper was accompanied by his wife and three children, all under school age, who were allowed on the stern deck and often strapped in to prevent them from falling into the canal. Boating families were never long enough in one place for children to attend school regularly, but, despite that, they were well cared for.

Flyboats were worked around the clock by three men, one of whom rested until they came to a lock. With the introduction of steam in the 1880s, the flyboat crews were increased to four. Boatmen could be away from home for weeks at a time. One Shipley boatman's daughter has recently reminisced:

> When we slept on the boat my mother had to 'barge up' for two families. My father had a large basket, in it would be four loaves, two flatcakes, 1lb of margarine, tea, 2lb of sugar, bacon, salt, marmalade and jam.

Usually a small cast iron stove was fixed in the middle of the boat's bulkhead, where simple meals were cooked and kettles boiled. Meals were prepared on the move and were not allowed to impede the boat's progress. Cabin space was restricted, headroom being no more than 4ft. Baking bread was not possible and there was much begging from cottages on the canal side. Boatmen carrying coal from Leeds down Airedale were known to barter food for small amounts of their cargo at canalside farmhouses. Most boatmen would keep a small dog and could turn their hands to poaching or petty thieving. There was little opportunity for recreation except for stoppages for drought or frost. When he was not preoccupied with his boat and its cargo the boatman lavished much of his time on his horse. Individual carriers tended to own their horses, although larger businesses, like the Walls, Oldfields and the Canal Company, provided them for their employees. Owner boatmen often had a stable attached to their home where hay and equipment were stored. Along the line of the canal several pubs kept stables where horses, food and smithy services were available at a small cost. The Company kept a large stable of horses at Bingley Five Rise when the flyboat service was introduced and 'dumb' boats were towed through each lock. A boatman was only as good as his horse and generally horses were well cared for by the bargees on the Leeds & Liverpool Canal. Our oral historian from Shipley recalls:

If you had a horse you always took that horse. That was your job, you had to look after it, keep it clean, see that it didn't get sore and feed it. My father, when he came to a lock, always put the food tin on the horse, so that it could be eating whilst the boat was going down the lock. The horse was always the first to be looked after. As soon as you got to the stables where you were stopping at night the horse was always dealt with before you made your supper, some straw into the stable, some bedding down for the night.

Each boat carried on its deck a provender tub or box of good quality fodder. Blacksmiths and horse doctors were located at regular intervals along the canal. The Canal Company were particularly considerate of their horses but towing forty- to fifty tons of coal, day in day out, inevitably took its toll on the horses, as this extract from the company archives confirms:

Date	Number/Type.	Cost.	Sale.	Service.	Reason for Disposal.	Purchaser.
Jan 1916	217 Black Gelding	£53	£12.	?	Worn out	J. Sutton
	287 Bay Mare	£40	£12	?	Unable to rise when down	J. Sutton
	425 Bay Gelding	£42	£12	2½yrs.	Canker in foot	J. Sutton
	206 Grey Gelding	£40	£14	?	WORN OUT	J. Sutton
	357 Bay Mare	£38	£30	4½yrs.	Non-layer down.	W.H.Hutchinson
Feb 7th.	412 Chestnut Mare.	£44	£30	3yrs.	Lame side bones	J. Sutton
	377 Bay Gelding	£30	£20	3yrs.	Contracted feet	J. Sutton.
March 7th.	416 Bay Mare	£42	£25	3 yrs.	Always in the Canal	Jas. Edge.
March 16th	258 Black Mare	£38	£1/5/4	?	Died at Wigan	Aldredge Bros
April	291 Black Mare	£40	£12	7½years	Worn out	James Edge.
May	256 Chestnut Gelding	£42	£5	?	Lame,& worn out	Sam Heath
July 1919	476 Bay Mare	£70	£1.	?	Pneumonia – Died	Liverpool Slaughter Hse.
Sept.	456 Bay Mare	£53	£1	?	Died in L'pool	
"	466 Chestnut	£52	£1	?	Died.Heart failure	at Wigan
Nov.	410 Brown Mare	£40	£1-10s	?	Twisted Bowels died.	
Dec.	489 Bay Mare	£95	£8.	9 months	Vicious – sold to J,Berry, drowned at Wigan.	
Feb20	524 Black Mare	£99	£1-5s	"	Drowned at Wigan.	

The following lists shows the date the Canal Company bought 19 horses between January 1916, and Dec 31 1920, purchased in Yorkshire, the length of service, or the reason for their disposal, during that period.

The main injuries were sores to the chest and shoulders as a result of ill-fitting collars and harnesses. A horse's length of service was not long and many simply died of exhaustion. When a boat ran aground or passed beneath a narrow bridge, horses could be dragged into the canal and drowned, unless there was a 'dogwash' nearby.

Boatmen, 1932. A rough, outspoken bunch of men who called a spade a shovel but who showed a strong sense of loyalty to the way of life that sustained them and particularly to the Leeds & Liverpool Company that employed them. Around 1914 they earned only £1 a week depending on the mileage and tonnage they did. Here, John Draper, Tommy Bower and the brothers John and Thomas Marsden, all of Latham, sport the traditional boatmen's costume of flat cap, corduroy trousers, knitted blue 'gansey' and clogs. In their old age the Company might find them a quiet lock to supervise.

Time to relax. Between loading and discharging cargoes, boatmen and horses took a well earned rest. It was at times like this that they enjoyed what little community life they had. There was little political consciousness or union organization among the boatmen. A favourable instrument was the melodeon which often accompanied one of the traditional clog dances. Clogs were preferred to wellingtons because they kept the deck cleaner. Here, a young boatman picks up a few tips from older heads aboard the *Uranus* at Manchester Ship Canal.

Mu at Buck Woods, Shipley, 1937. This diesel boat was built for Benjamin Walls Ltd in 1926. The bicycle allowed the mate to ride ahead and set locks and swing bridges for uninterrupted progress.

Canal Company barge *Tiger*, *c*.1900. This well known and familiar photograph of the horse drawn barge *Tiger* on the Leeds & Liverpool Canal at the turn of the twentieth century symbolizes barge life at that time. On deck is the ubiquitous dog kennel, horse provender and personally monogrammed water barrel, all freshly painted.

Omricon at Buck Woods swing bridge, 1938. A similar scene four decades later between Shipley and Leeds. During school holidays the boatmen would take all the family for the trip to Leeds Basin. This Canal Transport Company boat had recently left the wharf at Victoria Street, Shipley.

Teamwork. The old traditions of bargee life were strongest on the narrow boats which used a 'butty' boat – one drawn by another. The 'butty' was usually the responsibility of the boatman's wife but this system was not popular on the Leeds-Liverpool Canal. Even so, women played their part and here, on a cold winter's morning, Mrs Carrington is ready to help in her husband Tom's daily labours. Aboard not only did she handle the boat, but cooked, raised her children and doctored sick horses.

Mrs Bridges, a woman in a man's world. Mary Ellen Bridges worked on the boat *Alpha*. Once, single-handed, she took a full load through Gannow Tunnel at 9.20 p.m. on Friday and reputedly discharged her cargo at the Aire & Calder Navigation by 1.00 p.m. the next day, no doubt accompanied by the dog in the foreground.

Canal Community, *c*.1914. Some boatmen lived in self-contained communities alongside the canal like these waterside cottages in Culvert Lane, Newburgh.

A Canal Christening. A new generation of boatman is christened aboard his new home. In spite of the Canal Boat Act, barge children rarely attended school. They were, however, always well cared for, usually sleeping on the locker of what was called the 'spare side' of the boat.

'Sunday Best'. Many people used to bracket boatmen with the gypsy community. They were certainly a rough lot but many were Methodists or Salvationists. Several 'mission' houses built alongside the canal also catered for the boatmen's religious needs. One of these, a corrugated iron shack, was located near Jane Hills, Shipley. Here, a boatman and his wife are dressed in their Sunday best with their traditional pearly costumes. It was rare for boat people to marry outside the boating community.

Tow Horse. Young Dan Parr with a canal tow horse. Parr and his father both worked for H.&R. Ainscoughs, the canal carriers of Burscough. Larger beasts than this were required for the tough uplands of the Yorkshire Pennines. Clydesdales were preferred.

Tow Horse. A well-known photograph: here, the boatman leads his horse along the towpath in a hot Victorian summer. The lace ear muffs protected the horse from flies and the fodder basket enabled the horse to feed at locks and bridges while the boatmen attended to the canal machinery. In the background, the boat is of a clinker-built design, where individual planks of wood overlapped each other making them prone to damage at locks. By 1890 most wooden boats on the Leeds & Liverpool Canal were constructed to the carvel design, in which planks were laid adjacent to each other and then the joints were sealed (caulked).

Last Tow Horse on Canal. Tom Lamb leads away the tow horse of the very last working horse boat on the canal in 1960. This was the *Parbold*, owned by Ainscoughs and which supplied coal to their flour mills at Burscough and Parbold.

'Dogwash'. Occasionally a horse would get pulled into the canal. When this did occur, the horse simply swam along until it came to a canalside feature like this where it escaped by ramps set into the towpath. This one is close to the Leeds Basin with the railway arches to the right.

Billy Gelling, Skipton, *c.*1940. Gelling made his living by 'kebbing' coal, dropped from boats into the canal, by means of a bucket and a long stick. He then hawked it around the streets of Skipton at 6d a barrow load, as his predecessor Tommy Often had done the century before. Gelling lived at Waller Hill, near Thornton's staithe and boatyard, Skipton. He is reputed not to have worn a shirt. He's obviously had a good day here – his barrow is empty!

Springs Canal, *c.*1900. A unique picture showing (in the distance) a celebrated Skipton character called Tommy Often hauling a barge by his own strength the length of the Springs Canal, which he did for 6d a journey.

William Oldfield. Another very early private carrier on the Yorkshire side of the canal was William Oldfield (1821-1898) from Riddlesden. His father, of the same name, had mined for coal at Riddlesden since the mid-eighteenth century. He had helped to build the canal as a 'navvy' and became a boatman when it was finished. His son continued as a coal merchant, moving coal up and down the canal in a fleet of twenty boats.

Industry at Riddlesden. William Oldfield named many of his boats after family members, but here is the *Industry*, No.335, with a bulky load of stone at the pub-side wharf at Riddlesden. At one time, Oldfield owned a dozen horses at his Bank Lane Farm.

B.C. Walls & Co. Ltd, Skipton Basin. Once the Canal Company ceased carrying merchandise goods in 1921, three firms continued the trade and this was one of them with its head office at the Skipton Basin. Their very first boatman, Joe Salt, shows a young man how it's done.

The founder of Ben C. Walls Ltd, Ben Walls had replaced his father as a company employee in 1893 (after fifty years service at Higherland Lock, Gargrave). By 1903 he was the Leeds & Liverpool Traffic Inspector and in 1921 suddenly found himself out of a job. He immediately bought two steam flyboats, *Alpha* and *Beta* from his former employers and with his three sons commenced carrying as a bye-trader. Walls soon built up a fleet of twenty boats named after letters of the alphabet and the planets.

Joe Salt. Ben Walls immediately employed Joe Salt as his foreman. Salt claimed to have travelled and worked every canal in England, and here he is, aged eighty-five, when he finally stopped working the boats.

Iota, another of Wall's fleet. The *Iota* discharges her cargo of woollen bales at Shipley Wharf. Aboard is Tom Carrington known colloquially as 'Tommy Ninetoes'.

Walls Boats, *c*.1938. Here, several of Walls' boats, including the *Orb*, are laid up at East Marton owing to a burst culvert.

Fred Bateman, Skipton, 1947. Following the re-organization of the canal's maintenance in 1929, Fred Bateman became the senior inspector for the canal between Leeds and Blackburn, responsible for the supply of repair materials, dredging, water supply and ice-breaking. The last was a major headache for him in the long hard winter of 1947.

Company outing, 1895. In the summer of 1895 the Leeds & Liverpool Canal Company treated all their staff to a works trip. This photograph was taken at Whittle Springs at Johnson's Hillock, where there were pleasure gardens... and a brewery!

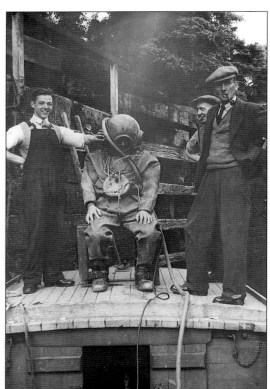

Stanley Wade. This long-serving company carpenter seen here, on the left, as a young man, assists a diver at the repair of Apperley Bridge Lock in the 1950s.

Theta at Burscough. This former Walls boat was purchased from Canal Transport Ltd by H.&R. Ainscough, flour millers (the mill is in background) of Burscough.

Eight
Industries and Trades along the Canal

The principal trades and goods which the early promoters of the canal anticipated carrying were essentially coal, limestone and general merchandise. Because of its high tollage, the last became the big money earner for the shareholders; coal was carried throughout the length of the canal and was its largest traffic throughout the canal's working life. Limestone, however, proved a disappointment in terms of increased traffic volume. These three dominated the early business of the canal but, as the decades passed and technologies changed, new industries appeared and not all of them were distributed by the railway network. After 1880 the canal's steam flyboat system allowed goods to be carried in small amounts to remote Pennine townships, sometimes for onward delivery. This was particularly true of the merchandise trade which came to include malt, hops, flour, oil, molasses, soap, paint, raisins, nuts and even gunpowder. As Lancashire and Yorkshire textile trades expanded, so did the business of the canal (imports and exports) in wool, cotton and flax. By the late nineteenth century new customers appeared in the shape of foundries, chemical works and engineering workshops. Even the horse droppings and street sweepings of Yorkshire's unsewered urban communities became a regular traffic on the canal and in demand by northern farmers. Up to 1850 about 50,000 tons of manure was carried annually on the canal and this had increased three fold by 1890.

A coal barge at Shipley Junction, *c*.1930. Coal has been the subject of countless pictures in this book. Here, a horse-drawn boat, with its three towing masts clearly shown, is moored on the Bradford Canal close to its junction with the Leeds & Liverpool Canal. The coal was craned out of the boat, dropped down the chute (in the distance) and into the wagons of a narrow gauge railway which passed beyond Windhill Lock for about half a mile towards Bradford.

Dubb Bridge, Bingley, *c.1935*. A coal boat docks alongside Victoria Mill, Dubb Bridge, across the canal from a stone masons yard supplied by Gilstead quarries. In the distance is the imposing spire of Mornington Road Church. The chimney in the centre of the photograph belongs to Britannia Mill, also alongside the canal.

A maintenance boat at Shipley Gasworks, *c.1960*. By the twentieth century, coal traffic along the canal remained buoyant owing to the demands of several urban gasworks like this one at Shipley.

Windhill Brickworks, c.1930. These were located between the Windhill quarry and the canal junction at Shipley. This and several other brickyards along the canal made use of the waterway for deliveries of coal to fire the kilns (two circular structures in centre) and to transport the bricks.

A lime kiln on the canal near Skipton. No one liked to transport quicklime so it was burned near to where it was required and several kiln sites are to be found close to the canal in Mid-Airedale, particularly between Riddlesden and Bingley. The Bradford Lime Kiln Company was commenced at the same time as the canal was built in the 1770s, but the main supplier of limestone and lime was the Earl of Thanet from his lime quarries, near Skipton Castle. This had been the reason for the Springs Canal in 1773.

Haw Bank Quarry, Embsay, *c.*1880. In 1785 the canal company leased the Skipton quarries from the Earl of Thanet and opened this quarry a mile from the canal. A tramway was built to link the two in 1794 but it ended 100ft above the branch canal where the limestone crashed noisily via long chutes into the waiting boats below.

Quarry tramway, Springs Canal, Skipton, *c.*1890. Eventually a new and less noisy tramway with an inclined plane was constructed in 1836, allowing the coal wagons to be tipped from a level just above the canal.

High Corn Mill, Springs Canal, 1890. A company flyboat loads with flour and grain at Skipton's ancient corn mill situated between the canal and Eller Beck. Flour was an important part of the Company's general merchandise trade from the very outset; several mills being located near or next to the canal on the Yorkshire side.

The canal basin, Victoria Street, Shipley, 1937. This relatively new warehouse had been built for Shipley's woollen trade and it is probably raw wool that is being delivered here by three boats including the *Tweed*, a motor flyboat belonging to Canal Transport Ltd, and the older horse boat the *Omega* (1905), formerly owned by Benjamin Walls but also a company boat by 1937.

Saltaire Mill, 1860. As textile production became mechanized, mills were deliberately re-sited alongside the canal. Benjamin Gott's mill at Armley was there from the outset. Perhaps the grandest example of this deliberate relocation was by Titus Salt, who took his theatre of operations out of Bradford and on to the main line of the canal in 1853. The print shows the canal running alongside the mill (top left) and disappearing behind the trees alongside the church (right). In the foreground beneath the bridge flows the River Aire.

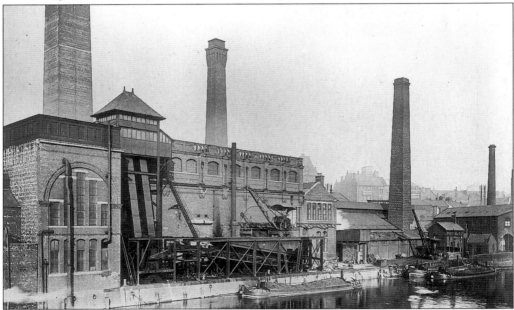

Whitehall Power Station, Leeds, c.1930. Power stations were attracted to the canal corridor for cooling water and coal supplies. In the 1920s power stations were built alongside the canal at Wigan, Whitebirk and Armley. This one, in the centre of Leeds, was built upstream from the Leeds Basin on the River Aire and to supply it with coal, an arm of the canal was built to join it.

Nine

Special Occasions and Events

This final section of the book is a pastiche of special events and occasions which have warranted the photographer's attention over the years. They have no real significance for the canal's development or prosperity but are, hopefully, sufficiently interesting of themselves to merit inclusion in this publication.

Sunday school outing, 1926. By 1900 several churches and schools were hiring canal boats for their annual summer excursion. Here, B.C. Walls' *Lambda* is ready to leave Skipton Wharf with a Sunday school party from Harrogate.

Although it was a 100-1 chance, the horse *Louis Quatorze* took it much to the dismay of Tommy Moloney, his jockey. Here the horse is in the Leeds & Liverpool Canal instead of in the Grand Sefton Steeplechase at Aintree in 1948. He was one of nine horses that did not finish the course but the only one to jump into the canal. Three years later the canal was screened off to prevent similar accidents.

A heavy load at Shipley, 1903. This huge boiler was on the last leg of its journey from Lancashire, destined for Shipley's new power station when it toppled into the canal and sank. It was salvaged and reloaded aboard Abraham Kendall's barge *Edith*.

Foulridge Tunnel tug timetable.

LEEDS AND LIVERPOOL CANAL CO.

NOTICE

FOULRIDGE TUNNEL

Alteration of working hours of Tug

On and after WEDNESDAY, APRIL 23rd, 1930, the Tug will leave when required :—

From the FOULRIDGE end of Tunnel:

MONDAY
TUESDAY | At the hours of 7 a.m., 9 a.m.,
WEDNESDAY | 11 a.m., 1 p.m., 3 p.m., and
THURSDAY | 5 p.m.
FRIDAY |

SATURDAY - 7 a.m., 9 a.m. and 11 a.m.

SUNDAY - - 10 a.m., if necessary

From the BARROWFORD end of the Tunnel:

MONDAY
TUESDAY
WEDNESDAY | At 8 a.m., 10 a.m., 12 noon, 2 p.m.,
THURSDAY | 4·0 p.m. and 6 p.m.
FRIDAY

SATURDAY - 8 a.m., 10 a.m. and 12 noon

SUNDAY - 11 a.m., if necessary

CANAL OFFICE, LIVERPOOL,
April 22nd, 1930.

ROBT. DAVIDSON,
General Manager and Engineer.

The cow that swam in Foulridge Tunnel, 1930. Perhaps this cow could not read the tunnel regulations when it fell into the canal at one end of the tunnel (1,640 yards) and swam the full length, to emerge at the other, none the worse for its misadventure.

VISIT HIRST FARM and THE WOODS
FOR A PLEASANT DAYS OUTING

Hirst Farm and Lock, c.1939. In the years after the First World War most people found more time and money for leisure. Several locations along the route of the canal became favourite venues for weekend and Bank Holiday pleasures. Farmer Whincup (far left) offered jugs of tea and home baked cakes to ramblers and visitors at his canalside farmhouse before 1939. Later, George Bagshaw also from here, was well known in Airedale for his home-made ice cream and bamboo fishing nets for 'tiddlers' in the canal. The line of the canal runs at the back of the farm and Hirst Lock is beyond the tree (far right).

Angling, c.1955. The canal as an amenity has become popular with several angling clubs. Here, members of Bradford Angling Club fish competitively at Hirst Wood, Shipley.

Fishin' int'cut. This time without a licence and in a more relaxed context. Bill King's photograph skilfully evokes those blue remembered days of childhood along the canal. The cat is obviously as optimistic as the lads.

The company motor launch *Victoria* passes the bridge at Elam Wood, Riddlesden, *c.*1900. On a hot summer's day like this the cool waters of the canal proved irresistible to these children, though the girls show a little more decorum than the boys!

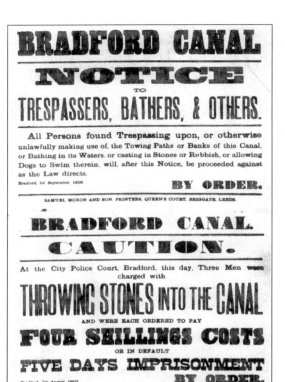

BRADFORD CANAL

NOTICE

TO

TRESPASSERS, BATHERS, & OTHERS.

All Persons found **Trespassing** upon, or otherwise
unlawfully making use of, the Towing Paths or Banks of this Canal,
or Bathing in its Waters, or casting in Stones or Rubbish, or allowing
Dogs to Swim therein, will, after this Notice, be proceeded against
as the Law directs.

Bradford, 1st September, 1906.

BY ORDER.

SAMUEL MOXON AND SON, PRINTERS, QUEEN'S COURT, BRIGGATE, LEEDS.

BRADFORD CANAL.

CAUTION.

At the City Police Court, Bradford, this day, Three Men were
charged with

THROWING STONES INTO THE CANAL

AND WERE EACH ORDERED TO PAY

FOUR SHILLINGS COSTS

OR IN DEFAULT

FIVE DAYS IMPRISONMENT

BY ORDER.

Bradford, 7th August, 1907.

B. Moxon and Son, Printers and Lithographers, Queen's Court, Briggate, Leeds.

Notice to canal bathers etc., 1906. The Canal Company, as early as 1842, had been anxious to monitor public behaviour along its towpaths by appointing its own police. They were particularly concerned about bathing, trespass and gambling and even pedal cyclists required a permit to use the towpath. Notices like this along the towpath discouraged a few and by 1900 the local constable was often responsible for reporting any misdemeanours.

Bathing at Hirst Wood, 1936. Swimming in the canal has always taken place, particularly by young people living close to the canal. This spot at Seven Arches, Hirst Wood, was a favourite with the youth of Saltaire and Shipley between the wars.

The canal bombed, 1939. At Maghull, near Liverpool, a swing bridge was completely wrecked during a German air raid in 1939. Here, company employees are repairing the bridge at full speed as barges were held up in and out of Liverpool.

'Bargee Belles'. As men left the Canal Company after 1939 to fight in the armed services, it became increasingly difficult to get labour to work on the boats and on the canal's maintenance. As a result boatmen's wages rose rapidly during the war as the amount of traffic on the canal increased. Young female volunteers from the Women's Land Army came forward for training on the boats. Here, the first contingent of girl bargees are with B.C. Walls aboard the *Venus* at Whitebirk.

The canal breach at Keighley, 1952. A sequence of dramatic photographs shows the serious breach of the canal bank near Booth Bridge, Keighley in May 1952. A torrent of thousands of gallons of water burst through the south bank of the canal alongside Keighley Golf Club wiping out two of its holes.

The Company maintenance boat was actually on the site at the time to investigate a known leak. In the second of these two photographs, the scale of the breach and the precarious position of the boat can be seen.

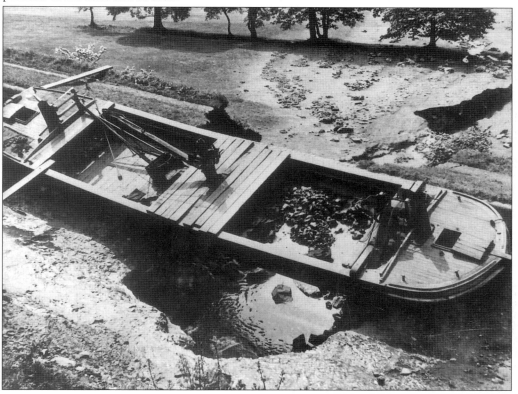

Chronology of the Leeds & Liverpool Canal

1698: An Act for making the Aire & Calder navigable.
1720. An Act for making the River Douglas navigable.
1766: Meeting at the Sun Inn, Bradford to discuss the proposed canal between Leeds and the West Coast.
1770: An Act for the canal from Leeds to Liverpool.
1770: The first sod cut at Halsall in Lancashire.
1771: An Act for a canal from Bradford to Shipley.
1772: The newly formed Leeds & Liverpool Canal Company bought a majority shareholding in the Douglas Navigation.
1774: Opening of Bradford Canal.
1775: Canal opened from Liverpool to Newburgh.
1775: John Longbotham resigned.
1777: Grand opening in Leeds of the Leeds to Holmbridge stretch.
1783: An Act allowing the L&LCC to purchase the River Douglas Navigation.
1789: Robert Whitworth reported on the cost of completing the canal, estimating £169,818, including a tunnel at Foulridge.
1790: Whitworth became engineer.
1790: An Act to authorize the raising of more money and making alterations to the line of the canal.
1791: Longbotham produced a deviation at the summit. He was opposed by Whitworth.
1794: An Act to vary the line of the navigation.
1796: Opening of Foulridge Tunnel.
1801: Longbotham died.
1801: Building of Gannow Tunnel and opening of the Foulridge to Henfield stretch.
1816: Main line completed. A flotilla travelled from Leeds to Liverpool.
1819: An Act for making the Leigh branch.
1821: Leigh branch completed.
1845: The L&LCC become carriers themselves.
1853: Twenty-one-year lease given to the London and North Western Railway Company for merchandize cargo.
1864: Southern end of the Lancaster Canal leased to the L&LCC for 999 years.
1921: Application to Parliament for the Abandonment of the Bradford Canal.
1923: The L&NW Railway Company and the Canal Company both bought by the LMS Railway Company.
1930: Three carrying companies amalgamated to form Canal Transport Ltd.
1948: Leeds & Liverpool Canal nationalized and later incorporated into the British Transport Board.
1963: The canal passed into the control of the British Waterways Board.

Acknowledgements

I owe a particular debt of gratitude to Mike Clarke, whose history and guide of the Leeds & Liverpool Canal has become the definitive work on the subject which no student should be without. Mike has been very generous in sharing with me his encyclopedic knowledge of the canal, its topography, technology and culture, as well as making available photographs and ephemera from his vast collection. I am also grateful to Geoff Wheat and David Lowe for their comments and corrections. David Lowe, as former managing director of Apollo Canal Carriers Ltd, has shared with me his vast working knowledge of the canal and its boats on the Yorkshire side.

My grateful thanks are also extended to all who loaned or supplied photographs for this book, in particular British Waterways; the Boat Museum at Ellesmere Port; North Yorkshire Libraries; Craven Museum, Skipton; Derek Lee; Joan Oldfield; Marjorie Baker; Geoff Wheat; Frank Woodall, Malcolm Hitt; Keighley Golf Club; Wilfred Wright; Eileen White; Agnes Walls.

Finally, my thanks go to Marlene Sharkey for her extremely useful secretarial help. Every effort has been made to trace the owners of copyright material but in some cases this has not proved possible. The author would be glad to hear from any further copyright owners of material reproduced in this publication.

Gary Firth, Wilsden, October 1999